Introduction

*Are we living in such human dependence
upon Jesus Christ that His life is being
manifested moment by moment?*

The essence of Oswald Chambers's classic devotional *My Utmost for His Highest* lies in asking the hard questions. For a man or woman to make a true, lasting commitment to the Lord of our salvation, Jesus Christ, much depends on answering honestly questions such as this one, questions that expose those worldly preservers—ego, pride, and envy.

Treasures from My Utmost for His Highest is a book of questions, yes, but there are also answers. Arranged topically, this collection of gems of inspiration and insight culled from Chambers's cherished bestseller has a priceless purpose: to enlighten readers and enable them to achieve the ultimate reward, eternal life.

The hard questions are only the beginning of giving—and living—one's utmost for His highest.

TREASURES
from My
UTMOST
for His
HIGHEST

Oswald Chambers

BARBOUR
PUBLISHING, INC.
Uhrichsville, Ohio

ISBN 1-57748-078-3

Unless otherwise noted, all Scripture quotations are taken from the Authorized King James Version of the Bible.

Published by Barbour Publishing, Inc.
P.O. Box 719
Uhrichsville, Ohio 44683
http://www.barbourbooks.com

Member of the
Evangelical Christian
Publishers Association

Printed in the United States of America.

Table of Contents

Abandonment

"But none of these things move me, neither count I my life dear unto myself." ACTS 20:24

Never consider whether you are of use; but ever consider that you are not your own but His.

"I will very gladly spend and be spent for you." 2 CORINTHIANS 12:15

We have no right in Christian work to be guided by our affinities; this is one of the biggest tests of our relationship to Jesus Christ. . . .
If we are abandoned to Jesus,
we have no ends of our own to serve.

"Lord, and what shall this man do? . . . What is that to thee? follow thou Me." JOHN 21:21-22

The mature stage is the life of a child which is never conscious;
we become so abandoned to God that the consciousness of being used never enters in.

Never consider whether you are of use; but ever consider that you are not your own but His.

Abandonment

Beware of stopping short of abandonment to God.

"Then Peter began to say unto Him, Lo, we have left all, and have followed Thee. . . ."
MARK 10:28

Beware of an abandonment which has the commercial spirit in it— "I am going to give myself to God because I want to be delivered from sin, because I want to be made holy. . . ."
We have got so commercialized
that we only go to God for something from Him, and not for Himself. . .
Beware of stopping short of abandonment to God.
Most of us know abandonment in vision only.

"Now when Simon Peter heard that it was the Lord, he girt his fisher's coat unto him. . . and did cast himself into the sea."
JOHN 21:7

Have you deliberately committed your will to Jesus Christ? It is a transaction of will, not of emotion; the emotion is simply the gilt-edge of the transaction. If you allow emotion first, you will never make the transaction.

Abandonment

*"Thy life will I give unto thee for a prey
in all places whither thou goest."*
JEREMIAH 45:5

When you do get through to abandonment to
God, you will be the most surprised
and delighted creature on earth. . . .

❧

"Come ye after Me." MARK 1:17

If you will give God your right to yourself,
He will make a holy experiment out of you.
God's experiments always succeed.

❧

*"And Peter. . .walked on the water, to go to Jesus.
But when he saw the wind boisterous,
he was afraid."*
MATTHEW 14:29-30

Whenever the realization of God comes in the
faintest way imaginable, recklessly abandon.
It is only by abandon that you recognize Him.

Atonement

*"Ought not Christ to have suffered these things,
and to enter into His glory?"* LUKE 24:26

Our Lord's Cross is the gateway into His life. . . .

*"And the Lord turned the captivity
of Job, when he prayed for his friends."*
JOB 42:10

I *cannot* make myself right with God,
I *cannot* make my life perfect;
I can only be right with God if I accept the
Atonement of the Lord Jesus Christ as an
absolute gift. Am I humble enough to accept it?

"In whom we have. . .the forgiveness of sins."
EPHESIANS 1:7

Forgiveness, which is so easy for us to accept, cost
the agony of Calvary. . . .When once you realize
all that it cost God to forgive you, you will be held
as in a vice, constrained by the love of God.

Atonement

"I have finished the work which Thou gavest Me to do." JOHN 17:4

The Death of Jesus Christ is the performance in history of the very Mind of God.

❧

"Walk while ye have the light, lest darkness come upon you." JOHN 12:35

Every bit of your life physical, moral and spiritual, is to be judged by the standard of the Atonement.

❧

"For by one offering he hath perfected for ever them that are sanctified." HEBREWS 10:14

It does not matter who or what we are, there is absolute reinstatement into God by the death of Jesus Christ and by no other way, not because Jesus Christ pleads, but because He died. It is not earned, but accepted.

Belief

To believe is to commit.

"My speech and my preaching
was not with enticing words."
1 CORINTHIANS 2:4

Belief in Jesus is a miracle produced
only by the efficacy of Redemption,
not by impressiveness of speech,
not by wooing and winning,
but by the sheer unaided power of God.

"Believest thou this?"
JOHN 11:26

To believe is to commit.

"Son of man, can these bones live?"
EZEKIEL 37:3

We would far rather work for God
than believe in Him.
Am I quite sure that God will
do what I cannot do?

Call of God

*"Whom shall I send, and who will go for us?
Then said I, Here am I; send me."*
ISAIAH 6:8

Get out of your mind the idea of expecting God
to come with compulsions and pleadings.

*"I heard the voice of the Lord, saying,
Whom shall I send?"* ISAIAH 6:8

As long as I consider my personal temperament
and think about what I am fitted for,
I shall never hear the call of God.
But when I am brought into relationship with
God, I am in the condition Isaiah was in.

*"But when it pleased God. . .to reveal
His Son in me. . . ."* GALATIANS 1:15-16

God gets me into a relationship with Himself
whereby I understand His call, then I do things
out of sheer love for Him on my own account.

15

Character

The final stage in the life of faith is attainment of character.

"He went out, not knowing whither he went."
HEBREWS 11:8

The final stage in the life of faith
is attainment of character.

*"Take now thy son. . .and offer him there
for a burnt offering upon one of
the mountains which I will tell thee of."*
GENESIS 22:2

Character determines how
a man interprets God's will (cf. Psalm 18:25-26).

*"In the year that king Uzziah died
I saw also the Lord."*
ISAIAH 6:1

My vision of God depends upon
the state of my character.
Character determines revelation.

Character

Remember that vision depends on character— the pure in heart see God.

"Blessed are the pure in heart:
for they shall see God."
MATTHEW 5:8

Remember that vision depends on character—
the pure in heart see God.

"The Lord . . . hath sent me,
that thou mightest receive thy sight."
ACTS 9:17

The abiding characteristic of a spiritual man is
the interpretation of the Lord Jesus Christ
to himself, and the interpretation to others
of the purposes of God.

"Come up hither, and I will shew thee things."
REVELATION 4:1

God has to hide from us what He does
until by personal character we get to
the place where He can reveal it.

Chastening

"And Samuel feared to shew Eli the vision."
1 SAMUEL 3:15

Chastening is more than a means of discipline,
it is meant to get me to the place of saying,
"Speak, Lord."

*"If thou hadst known. . .in this thy day, the things
which belong unto thy peace! but now they are
hid from thine eyes."* LUKE 19:42

Never be afraid when God brings back the past.
Let memory have its way. It is a minister of God
with its rebuke and chastisement and sorrow.

*"Despise not thou the chastening of the Lord, nor
faint when thou art rebuked of Him."*
HEBREWS 12:5

It is very easy to quench the Spirit; we do it by
despising the chastening of the Lord, by fainting
when we are rebuked by Him.

Choices

"I am made all things to all men,
that I might by all means save some."
1 CORINTHIANS 9:22

We are not workers for God by choice.
Many people deliberately choose to be workers,
but they have no matter in them of God's
almighty grace, no matter of His mighty word.

"If thou wilt take the left hand,
then I will go to the right;
or if thou depart to the right hand,
then I will go to the left."
GENESIS 13:9

Whenever *right* is made the guidance in the life,
it will blunt the spiritual insight. . .
Many of us do not go on spiritually
because we prefer to choose what is right instead
of relying on God to choose for us.

Circumstances

"And Samuel feared to shew Eli the vision."
1 SAMUEL 3:15

Get into the habit of saying, "Speak, Lord,"
and life will become a romance.
Every time circumstances press, say,
"Speak, Lord"; make time to listen.

"Behold, the hour cometh. . .
that ye shall be scattered."
JOHN 16:32

Spiritual grit is what we need.

"Labourers together with God."
1 CORINTHIANS 3:9

We have no right to judge where we should be
put, or to have preconceived notions as to what
God is fitting us for. God engineers everything. . .

Circumstances

*"All things work together for good
to them that love God."*
ROMANS 8:28

All your circumstances are in the hand of God,
therefore never think it strange concerning
the circumstances you are in.

"Take no thought for your life." *MATTHEW 6:25*

Jesus Christ knows our circumstances
better than we do. . . .

*"Ye are they which have continued
with Me in My temptations."*
LUKE 22:28

We have the idea that we ought to shield
ourselves from some of the things God brings
round us. Never! God engineers circumstances and
whatever they may be like we have to see that we
face them while abiding continually with Him.

*All your
circumstances
are in
the hand
of God.*

Coming to Christ

*If you want to
know how real
you are,
test yourself by
these words
"Come unto
Me."*

"Come unto Me."
MATTHEW 11:28

If I will come to Jesus my actual life will
be brought into accordance with my real desires;
I will actually cease from sin,
and actually find the song of the Lord begin.

"Come unto Me."
MATTHEW 11:28

The attitude of coming is that the will
resolutely lets go of everything and
deliberately commits all to Him.

"Come unto Me."
MATTHEW 11:28

If you want to know how real you are,
test yourself by these words
"Come unto Me."

Concentration on God

"And Samuel feared to shew Eli the vision."
1 SAMUEL 3:15

Never ask the advice of another about anything
God makes you decide before Him.

"Look unto Me, and be ye saved." ISAIAH 45:22

Narrow all your interests until the attitude
of mind and heart and body is
concentration on Jesus Christ.

*"But the high places were not taken away out of
Israel: nevertheless the heart of Asa was perfect
all his days." 2 CHRONICLES 15:17*

You no more need a holiday from
spiritual concentration than your heart needs
a holiday from beating. . . .
God wants you to be entirely His,
and this means that you have to
watch to keep yourself fit.

*Narrow all
your interests
until the
attitude of
mind and heart
and body is
concentration
on Jesus
Christ.*

Concentration on God

Jesus says that there is only one way to develop spiritually, and that is by concentration on God.

"Behold the fowls of the air...
Consider the lilies of the field."
MATTHEW 6:26, 28

Jesus says that there is only one way to develop spiritually, and that is by concentration on God.

"But seek ye first the kingdom of God,
and His righteousness;
and all these things shall be added unto you."
MATTHEW 6:33

Jesus taught that a disciple has to make his relationship to God the dominating concentration of his life, and to be carefully careless about everything else in comparison to that.

"The friend of the bridegroom."
JOHN 3:29

Christian work may be a means of evading the soul's concentration on Jesus Christ.

Conscience

*"Stand fast therefore in the liberty wherewith
Christ hath made us free."*
GALATIANS 5:1

*Conscience is
that faculty in
me which
attaches itself
to the highest
that I know.*

There is only one liberty,
the liberty of Jesus at work in our conscience
enabling us to do what is right.

❧

*"A conscience void of offence toward God,
and toward men."*
ACTS 24:16

Conscience is that faculty in me which attaches
itself to the highest that I know, and tells me what
the highest I know demands that I do.

❧

Crisis

He brings us to the place where He asks us to be our utmost for Him.

"I have finished the work which Thou gavest Me to do."
JOHN 17:4

There are very few crises in life;
the great crisis is the surrender of the will.

*"My eager desire and hope being
that I may never feel ashamed,
but that now as ever I may do honour to
Christ in my own person by fearless courage."*
PHILIPPIANS 1:20 (MOFFAT)

He brings us to the place where He asks us
to be our utmost for Him,
and we begin to debate;
then He produces a providential crisis
where we have to decide—
for or against,
and from that point the "Great Divide" begins.

*It is
when a
crisis arises
that we
instantly
reveal
upon whom
we rely.*

"I am crucified with Christ" GALATIANS 2:20

If you are up against the question
of relinquishing, go through the crisis,
relinquish all, and God will make you fit
for all that He requires of you.

"Why are ye fearful, O ye of little faith?"
MATTHEW 8:26

It is when a crisis arises that we instantly
reveal upon whom we rely.

"When thou wast under the fig tree, I saw thee."
JOHN 1:48

Crises always reveal character.

The Cross

There is nothing more certain in Time or Eternity than what Jesus Christ did on the Cross.

"And when He is come,
He will convict the world of sin. . . ."
JOHN 16:8 (RV)

It is shallow nonsense to say that
God forgives us because He is love. . . .
The love of God means Calvary, and nothing less;
the love of God is spelt on the Cross
and nowhere else.

"Who His own self bare
our sins in His own body on the tree."
1 PETER 2:24

The Cross was a superb triumph in which
the foundations of hell were shaken.
There is nothing more certain in Time or Eternity
than what Jesus Christ did on the Cross:
He switched the whole of the human race
back into a right relationship with God.

The Cross

*"But God forbid that I should glory,
save in the cross of our Lord Jesus Christ."*
GALATIANS 6:14

If we get away from brooding on the tragedy
of God upon the Cross in our preaching
it produces nothing.
It does not convey the energy of God to man;
it may be interesting but it has no power.
But preach the Cross,
and the energy of God is let loose.

*"I, if I be lifted up from the earth,
will draw all men unto Me."*
JOHN 12:32

The one thing we have to do
is to exhibit Jesus Christ crucified,
to lift Him up all the time.
Every doctrine that is not imbedded in the
Cross of Jesus will lead astray.

*The one thing
we have to do
is to exhibit
Jesus Christ
crucified,
to lift Him up
all the time.*

Darkness

The only possibility of understanding the teaching of Jesus is by the light of the Spirit of God on the inside.

"Clouds and darkness are round about Him."
PSALM 97:2

The only possibility of understanding
the teaching of Jesus is by the light of
the Spirit of God on the inside.

"What I tell you in darkness, that speak ye in light: and what ye hear in the ear, that preach ye upon the housetops." MATTHEW 10:27

After every time of darkness there comes
a mixture of delight and humiliation. . .
delight in hearing God speak,
but chiefly humiliation—
What a long time I was in hearing that!

"Behold, He cometh with clouds." REVELATION 1:7

Is there anyone "save Jesus only" in your cloud?
If so, it will get darker; you must get to the place
where there is "no one any more save Jesus only."

Darkness

"Therefore if thou bring thy gift to the altar, and there rememberest that thy brother hath ought against thee; leave there thy gift before the altar, and go thy way; first be reconciled to thy brother, and then come and offer thy gift."
MATTHEW 5:23-24

Have you anything to hide from God? If you have, then let God search you with His light.

"If any man will do His will, he shall know of the doctrine. . . ." JOHN 7:17

Intellectual darkness comes through ignorance; spiritual darkness comes because of something I do not intend to obey.

Dependence on God

It is the saddest thing to see people in the service of God depending on that which the grace of God never gave them.

"Behold, as the eyes of servants look
unto the hand of their masters. . .
so our eyes wait upon the Lord our God."
PSALM 123:2

The danger is lest no longer relying on God
you ignore the lifting up of your eyes to Him.

"All my fresh springs shall be in Thee."
PSALM 87:7 (PBV)

It is the saddest thing to see people in the service
of God depending on that which the grace of God
never gave them, depending on what
they have by the accident of heredity.

"Father, I thank Thee that Thou hast heard Me."
JOHN 11:41

Are we living in such human dependence
upon Jesus Christ that His life is being
manifested moment by moment?

Dependence on God

"Will ye also go away?"
JOHN 6:67

. . . .Live a natural life of
absolute dependence on Jesus Christ.
Never try to live the life with God
on any other line than God's line,
and that line is absolute devotion to Him.

"Lord, and what shall this man do?. . .
What is that to thee? Follow thou Me."
JOHN 21:21-22

A saint is never consciously a saint;
a saint is consciously dependent on God.

"He went out, not knowing whither he went."
HEBREWS 11:8

God does not tell you what He is going to do;
He reveals to you Who He is.

Devotion

One life wholly devoted to God is of more value to God than one hundred lives simply awakened by His Spirit.

"Thomas answered and said unto Him, My Lord and my God."
JOHN 20:28

Are we being more devoted to service than to Jesus Christ?

"I have appeared unto thee for this purpose."
ACTS 26:16

Paul was devoted to a Person not to a cause.

"Notwithstanding in this rejoice not, that the spirits are subject unto you."
LUKE 10:20

One life wholly devoted to God is of more value to God than one hundred lives simply awakened by His Spirit.

Devotion

"Lovest thou Me?. . . Feed My sheep." JOHN 21:16

People do not want to be devoted to Jesus, but only to the cause He started. Jesus Christ is a source of deep offense to the educated mind of today that does not want Him in any other way than as a Comrade.

We have to battle through our moods into absolute devotion to the Lord Jesus.

"For His name's sake they went forth." 3 JOHN 7

The men and women Our Lord sends out on His enterprises are the ordinary human stuff, plus dominating devotion to Himself wrought by the Holy Ghost.

"The Son of God, who loved me, and gave Himself for me." GALATIANS 2:20

We have to battle through our moods into absolute devotion to the Lord Jesus, to get out of the hole-and-corner business of our experience into abandoned devotion to Him.

Difficulty

God is the Master Engineer, He allows the difficulties to come in order to see if you can vault over them properly. . . .

"Take now thy son. . . ." GENESIS 22:2

If God has made your cup sweet,
drink it with grace; if He has made it bitter,
drink it in communion with Him. . . .
In the crucible you learn to know God better.

*"That ye may know what is the hope
of His calling. . . ."* EPHESIANS 1:18

God is the Master Engineer,
He allows the difficulties to come in order to see
if you can vault over them properly. . . .

*"How much more shall your Father which is in
heaven give good things to them that ask Him?"*
MATTHEW 7:11

Notion your mind with the idea that God is there.
If once the mind is notioned along that line,
then when you are in difficulties it is as easy
as breathing to remember—
Why, my Father knows all about it!

Discernment

Discernment is God's call to intercession, never to fault finding.

"A conscience void of offence toward God, and toward men." ACTS 24:16

He does not come with a voice like thunder;
His voice is so gentle that it is easy to ignore it.

"Praying always with all prayer and supplication in the Spirit." EPHESIANS 6:18

Discernment is God's call to intercession,
never to fault finding.

"If ye know these things, happy are ye if ye do them." JOHN 13:17

When you know you should do a thing, and do it,
immediately you know more.

"The simplicity that is in Christ." 2 CORINTHIANS 11:3

Immediately we obey, we discern.

Discernment

Your part is to be so rightly related to God that His discernment comes through you all the time for the blessing of another soul.

"If any man see his brother sin a sin which is not unto death, he shall ask, and He shall give him life for them that sin not unto death."
JOHN 5:16

If we are not heedful of the way the Spirit of God works in us, we will become spiritual hypocrites. We see where other folks are failing, and we turn our discernment into the gibe of criticism instead of into intercession on their behalf.

"Lord, what shall this man do? . . . What is that to thee? Follow thou Me."
JOHN 21:21-22

When you do have to give advice to another, God will advise through you with the direct understanding of His Spirit; your part is to be so rightly related to God that His discernment comes through you all the time for the blessing of another soul.

Discipleship

Discipleship is based on devotion to Jesus Christ.

"Go ye therefore, and teach [disciple] all nations."
MATTHEW 28:19

You cannot make disciples unless
you are a disciple yourself.

&

*"Notwithstanding in this rejoice not,
that the spirits are subject unto you."*
LUKE 10:20

. . .We are not to save souls, but to disciple them.
Salvation and sanctification are the work
of God's sovereign grace;
our work as His disciples is to disciple lives
until they are wholly yielded to God.

&

"Lovest thou Me?. . . Feed My sheep."
JOHN 21:16

Discipleship is based on devotion to Jesus Christ,
not on adherence to a belief or a creed.

Discipleship

*"For which of you, intending to build a tower,
sitteth not down first, and counteth the cost,
whether he have sufficient to finish it?"*
LUKE 14:28

Our Lord implies that the only men and women
He will use in His building enterprises
are those who love Him
personally, passionately and devotedly
beyond any of the closest ties on earth.
The conditions are stern, but they are glorious.

"Thine they were, and Thou gavest them Me."
JOHN 17:6

Our Lord makes a disciple His own possession.

"Woe is unto me, if I preach not the gospel!"
1 CORINTHIANS 9:16

Discipleship has an option with it—
"If any man. . . ."

Discipline

"Enter ye in at the strait gate. . . because strait is the gate, and narrow is the way. . . ." MATTHEW 7:13-14

It takes a tremendous amount of discipline to live the noble life of a disciple of Jesus in actual things. It is always necessary to make an effort to be noble.

"Abraham had two sons, the one by a bondmaid, the other by a freewoman." GALATIANS 4:22

We go wrong because we stubbornly refuse to discipline ourselves, physically, morally or mentally. . . .You must discipline yourself now. If you do not, you will ruin the whole of your personal life for God.

"Bringing into captivity every thought to the obedience of Christ." 2 CORINTHIANS 10:5

True earnestness is found in obeying God, not in the inclination to serve Him that is born of undisciplined human nature.

41

Discouragement

Beware of the satisfaction of sinking back and saying— "It can't be done"; you know it can be done if you look to Jesus.

"Moses. . .went out unto his brethren, and looked on their burdens."
EXODUS 2:11

If you are going through a time of discouragement, there is a big personal enlargement ahead.

"And when he heard this, he was very sorrowful: for he was very rich."
LUKE 18:23

Discouragement is disenchanted self-love, and self-love may be love of my devotion to Jesus.

"From whence then hast Thou that living water?"
JOHN 4:11

Beware of the satisfaction
of sinking back and saying—
"It can't be done";
you know it can be done if you look to Jesus.

Doubt

*"Stand fast therefore in the liberty wherewith
Christ hath made us free."*
GALATIANS 5:1

We are not asked to believe the Bible,
but to believe the One Whom the Bible reveals
(cf. John 5:39-40).

"Your life is hid with Christ in God."
COLOSSIANS 3:3

The most precarious thing is to try and live
without God.

*"If Thou canst do any thing,
have compassion on us, and help us."*
MARK 9:22

It takes the valley of humiliation to root
the skepticism out of us.

Drudgery

"And beside this. . .add. . . ." 2 PETER 1:5

There are times when there is no illumination
and no thrill, but just the daily round,
the common task. Routine is God's way of
saving us between our times of inspiration.

*"If I then, your Lord and Master,
have washed your feet;
ye also ought to wash one another's feet."
JOHN 13:14*

Can I use a towel as He did?. . .
It takes God Almighty Incarnate in us to do
the meanest duty as it ought to be done.

*"For He hath said, 'I will never leave thee,
nor forsake thee.' " HEBREWS 13:5*

Sometimes it is not difficulty that makes me think
God will forsake me, but drudgery.

Drudgery

*". . . .in much patience, in afflictions,
in necessities, in distresses."* 2 CORINTHIANS 6:4

It takes Almighty grace to take the next step
when there is no vision and no spectator—
the next step in devotion,
the next step in your study, in your reading,
in your kitchen; the next step in your duty.

*"Except a man be born again,
he cannot see the kingdom of God."*
JOHN 3:3

Sometimes we are fresh for a prayer meeting but
not fresh for cleaning boots!

"Arise, shine." ISAIAH 60:1

Drudgery is work that is very far removed
from anything to do with the ideal—
the utterly mean grubby things;
and when we come in contact with them we know
instantly whether or not we are spiritually real.

Duty

"Pray ye therefore the Lord of the harvest, that He will send forth labourers into His harvest."
MATTHEW 9:38

No Christian has a special work to do. . .
Our Lord calls to no special work:
He calls to Himself.

"Feed my sheep." JOHN 21:17

If I love my Lord I have no business to
be guided by natural temperament;
I have to feed His sheep.
There is no relief and no release
from this commission.

*"But we trusted. . .and beside all this,
to day is the third day. . . ."* LUKE 24:21

If we will do the duty that lies nearest,
we shall see Him. . . .It is in the commonplace
things that the Deity of Jesus Christ is realized.

Eternal Life

"Death hath no more dominion over Him . . .
in that He liveth,
He liveth unto God.
Likewise reckon ye also yourselves
to be dead indeed unto sin,
but alive unto God."
ROMANS 6:9-11

Eternal Life has nothing to do with Time,
it is the life which Jesus lived
when He was down here.
The only source of Life is the Lord Jesus Christ.

The real meaning of eternal life is a life that can face anything it has to face without wavering.

"Because thou hast kept the word
of My patience."
REVELATION 3:10

The real meaning of eternal life is a life that can
face anything it has to face without wavering.

Faith

"He went out, not knowing whither he went."
HEBREWS 11:8

Faith never knows where it is being led,
but it loves and knows the One Who is leading.
It is a life *of faith*, not of intellect and reason,
but a life of knowing Who makes us "go."
The root of faith is the knowledge of a Person,
and one of the biggest snares is the idea that
God is sure to lead us to success.

*"We have received. . .the spirit which is of God;
that we might know the things that are freely
given to us of God."* 1 CORINTHIANS 2:12

Faith that is sure of itself is not faith;
faith that is sure of God is the only faith there is.

"Because thou hast kept the word of My patience."
REVELATION 3:10

Faith is the heroic effort of your life; you fling
yourself in reckless confidence on God.

Faith

*Faith is
not in
what Jesus
says but in
Himself...*

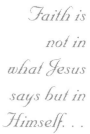

*"And my speech and my preaching was not
with enticing words of man's wisdom, but in
demonstration of the Spirit and of power."*
I CORINTHIANS 2:4

If your faith is in experiences, anything that
happens is likely to upset that faith;
but nothing can ever upset God or
the almighty Reality of Redemption.

"Faith as a grain of mustard seed. . . ."
MATTHEW 17:20

"Though He slay me, yet will I trust Him"—
this is the most sublime utterance of faith
in the whole of the Bible.

"Lord, that I may receive my sight." LUKE 18:41

Faith is not in what Jesus says but in Himself;
if we only look at what He says we shall never
believe. When once we see Jesus, He does the
impossible thing as naturally as breathing.

Faith

Stand off in faith believing that what Jesus said is true. . .

"Said I not unto thee, that, if thou wouldest believe, thou shouldest see the glory of God?"
JOHN 11:40

Faith must be tested, because it can be turned into a personal possession only through conflict. What is your faith up against just now?

"Said I not unto thee, that, if thou wouldest believe, thou shouldest see the glory of God?"
JOHN 11:40

There is continual testing in the life of faith, and the last great test is death.

"Ye know not what ye ask."
MATTHEW 20:22

Stand off in faith believing that what Jesus said is true, though in the meantime you do not understand what God is doing.

"The Son of God, who loved me,
and gave Himself for me."
GALATIANS 2:20

All our fears are wicked, and we fear because we
will not nourish ourselves in our faith.
How can anyone who is identified with
Jesus Christ suffer from doubt or fear!

"He hath said. . .so that we may boldly say. . . ."
HEBREWS 13:5-6

It does not matter what evil or wrong may be in
the way, He has said—"I will never leave thee."

. . .we fear
because we
will not
nourish
ourselves
in our faith.

51

Following Jesus

"Peter said unto Him, 'Lord,
why cannot I follow Thee now?' "
JOHN 13:37

Never run before God's guidance. If there is the
slightest doubt, then He is not guiding.
Whenever there is doubt—*don't.*

"Whither I go, thou canst not follow Me now;
but thou shalt follow Me afterwards."
JOHN 13:36

When we have come to the end of ourselves,
not in imagination but really,
we are able to receive the Holy Spirit.

Friendship With God

"He must increase, but I must decrease." JOHN 3:30

If you become a necessity to a soul, you are out of God's order. As a worker, your great responsibility is to be a friend of the Bridegroom.

❧

"Have I been so long time with you, and yet hast thou not known Me?" JOHN 14:9

Friendship is rare on earth. It means identity in thought and heart and spirit. The whole discipline of life is to enable us to enter into this closest relationship with Jesus Christ.

❧

"The secret [friendship, RV] of the Lord is with them that fear Him." PSALM 25:14

What is the sign of a friend? That he tells you secret sorrows? No, that he tells you secret joys . . . .Have we ever let God tell us any of His joys, or are we telling God our secrets so continually that we leave no room for Him to talk to us?

The whole discipline of life is to enable us to enter into this closest relationship with Jesus Christ.

Grace

"And whosoever shall compel thee to go a mile, go with him twain."
MATTHEW 5:41

God does not ask us to do the things that are easy to us naturally; He only asks us to do the things we are perfectly fitted to do by His grace.

"Partakers of the divine nature."
2 PETER 1:4

Learn to lavish the grace of God on others.

"We. . .beseech you also that ye receive not the grace of God in vain."
2 CORINTHIANS 6:1

The grace you had yesterday will not do for today. Grace is the overflowing favour of God; you can always reckon it is there to draw upon.

Guidance

*We have to
be so one
with God that
we do not
continually
need to ask
for guidance.*

"Choose you this day whom ye will serve."
JOSHUA 24:15

You have no business to find out
where God is leading, the only thing God will
explain to you is Himself.

❧

"I being in the way, the Lord led me. . . ."
GENESIS 24:27

We have to be so one with God that we do not
continually need to ask for guidance.

❧

*"They that wait upon the Lord. . .
shall walk, and not faint."*
ISAIAH 40:31

If our common-sense decisions are not His order,
He will press through them and check;
then we must be quiet and wait
for the direction of His presence.

Habit

The right thing to do with habits is to lose them in the life of the Lord.

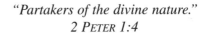

"Partakers of the divine nature."
2 PETER 1:4

. . .The first habit to form is the habit of realizing the provision God has made.

"For if these things are yours and abound, they make you to be not idle nor unfruitful."
2 PETER 1:8 (RV)

The right thing to do with habits is to lose them in the life of the Lord.

"His servants ye are to whom ye obey."
ROMANS 6:16

It is easy to sing—"He will break every fetter" and at the same time be living a life of obvious slavery to yourself. Yielding to Jesus will break every form of slavery in any human life.

Hearing God

Jesus Christ says a great deal that we listen to, but do not hear. . .

*"Yet lackest thou one thing;
sell all that thou hast. . .and come, follow Me."*
LUKE 18:22

Jesus Christ says a great deal that we listen to,
but do not hear; when we do hear,
His words are amazingly hard.

*"But we trusted. . .and beside all this,
to day is the third day. . . ."*
LUKE 24:21

Lust means—I must have it at once. Spiritual lust
makes me demand an answer from God,
instead of seeking God Who gives the answer.

*"Lord, I will follow Thee
whithersoever Thou goest."*
LUKE 9:57

The words of the Lord hurt and offend until
there is nothing left to hurt or offend.

Hearing God

We like to
listen to
personal
testimonies,
but we do not
desire that
God Himself
should speak
to us.

*"And they said unto Moses,
'Speak thou with us, and we will hear:
but let not God speak with us, lest we die.' "*
EXODUS 20:19

We show how little we love God
by preferring to listen to His servants only.
We like to listen to personal testimonies,
but we do not desire that God Himself
should speak to us.

"Speak; for Thy servant heareth."
1 SAMUEL 3:10

A lily, or a tree, or a servant of god,
may convey God's message to me
What hinders me from hearing is that
I am taken up with other things.
It is not that I will not hear God,
but I am not devoted in the right place.
I am devoted to things,
to service, to convictions,
and God may say what He likes
but I do not hear Him.

Holiness

The destined
end of man is
not happiness,
nor health,
but holiness.

"Ye shall be holy; for I am holy."
1 PETER 1:16 (RV)

Continually restate to yourself
what the purpose of your life is.
The destined end of man is not happiness,
nor health, but holiness.

"The friend of the bridegroom."
JOHN 3:29

If my holiness is not drawing towards Him,
it is not holiness of the right order,
but an influence that will awaken inordinate
affection and lead souls away into side eddies.

"To him that overcometh. . . ."
REVELATION 2:7

Holiness is the balance between my disposition
and the law of God as expressed in Jesus Christ.

Holy Spirit

The
Holy Spirit is
the One Who
makes real
in you all
that Jesus did
for you.

*"Tarry ye in the city of Jerusalem,
until ye be endued with power from on high."*
LUKE 24:49

The Holy Spirit's influence and power were at
work before Pentecost, but *He* was not there.
Immediately Our Lord was glorified in
Ascension, the Holy Spirit came into this world,
and He has been here ever since.

"For every one that asketh receiveth." LUKE 11:10

The Holy Spirit is the One Who makes real
in you all that Jesus did for you.

*"For if we have been planted together
in the likeness of His death, we shall be also in
the likeness of His resurrection."*
ROMANS 6:5

The Holy Spirit cannot be located as a Guest
in a house, He invades everything.

Holy Spirit

"Verily I say unto thee,
Thou shalt by no means come out thence,
till thou hast paid the uttermost farthing."
MATTHEW 5:26

God is determined to make you
pure and holy and right;
He will not allow you to escape for one moment
from the scrutiny of the Holy Spirit.

"We know not what we
should pray for as we ought:
but the Spirit itself maketh intercession for us
with groanings which cannot be uttered."
ROMANS 8:26

God searches your heart
not to know what your conscious prayers are,
but to find out what is the prayer
of the Holy Spirit.

God searches
your heart
. . .to find out
what is
the prayer
of the
Holy Spirit.

Human Nature

*He trusted
absolutely in
what He could
do for the
human race.*

"Did not our heart burn within us?"
LUKE 24:32

Much of our distress as Christians
comes not because of sin,
but because we are ignorant
of the laws of our own nature.

"Son of man, can these bones live?"
EZEKIEL 37:3

When God wants to show you
what human nature is like apart from Himself,
He has to show it you in yourself.

"This is your hour, and the power of darkness."
LUKE 22:53

Jesus Christ never trusted human nature,
yet He was never cynical,
because He trusted absolutely in what
He could do for the human race.

Humility

"Humble yourself"— it is a humbling business to knock at God's door.

"Seek, and ye shall find."
LUKE 11:9

"Humble yourself"—
it is a humbling business to knock at God's door
—you have to knock with the crucified thief.

*"Whatsoever ye do,
do all to the glory of God."*
1 CORINTHIANS 10:31

It takes Almighty God Incarnate in us to do the
meanest duty to the glory of God.

*"For with what judgment ye judge,
ye shall be judged;
and with what measure ye mete,
it shall be measured to you again."*
MATTHEW 7:2

The great characteristic of a saint is humility. . . .

Humility

The real test of the saint is not preaching the gospel, but washing disciple's feet.

"I am crucified with Christ; nevertheless I live; yet not I, but Christ liveth in me."
GALATIANS 2:20

The passion of Christianity is that I deliberately sign away my own rights and become a bondslave of Jesus Christ.

"Though the more abundantly I love you, the less I be loved."
2 CORINTHIANS 12:15

The real test of the saint is not preaching the gospel, but washing disciples' feet.

"Master, where dwellest Thou?. . . Come and see. . . .Follow Me."
JOHN 1:38-39, 43

Humility before men may be unconscious blasphemy before God.

Individuality

"Fellow labourer in the gospel of Christ."
1 THESSALONIANS 3:2

As long as you have a personal interest
in your own character, or any set ambition,
you cannot get through into identification
with God's interests.

*"If any man will come after Me,
let him deny himself."*
MATTHEW 16:24

It is the continual assertion
of individuality that hinders our
spiritual life more than anything else.
If you say—"I cannot believe,"
it is because individuality is in the road;
individuality never can believe.
Personality cannot help believing.

*It is the
continual
assertion of
individuality
that hinders
our spiritual
life more than
anything else.*

65

Initiative

The initiative of the saint is not towards self-realization, but towards knowing Jesus Christ.

"Add to your faith virtue. . ."
("Furnish your faith with resolution," MOFFAT)
2 PETER 1:5

Beware of the tendency of asking the way
when you know it perfectly well.
Take the initiative, stop hesitating,
and take the first step.

"That I may know Him."
PHILIPPIANS 3:10

The initiative of the saint
is not towards self-realization,
but towards knowing Jesus Christ.

"Arise from the dead."
EPHESIANS 5:14

God does not give us overcoming life;
He gives us life as we overcome.

Initiative

"Arise, let us go hence."
JOHN 14:31

Dreaming about a thing
in order to do it properly is right;
but dreaming about it when
we should be doing it is wrong.

*"Let us consider one another
to provoke unto love and to good works;
not forsaking the assembling
of ourselves together."*
HEBREWS 10:24-25

The note struck in Hebrews 10 is that of
provoking one another and of keeping together—
both of which require initiative,
the initiative of Christ realization,
not of self-realization.

*God does
not give us
overcoming
life; He gives
us life as we
overcome.*

Intercession

The real business of your life as a saved soul is intercessory prayer. . .

"And the Lord turned the captivity of Job, when he prayed for his friends."
JOB 42:10

The real business of your life
as a saved soul is intercessory prayer. . . .
Pray for your friends *now*;
pray for those with whom you come in contact *now*.

"Praying always with all prayer and supplication in the Spirit." EPHESIANS 6:18

It is impossible to intercede vitally
unless we are perfectly sure of God,
and the greatest dissipator of our relationship to
God is personal sympathy and personal prejudice.

"And He. . .wondered that there was no intercessor." ISAIAH 59:16

Worship and intercession must go together,
the one is impossible without the other.

Intercession

*The thing
to watch in
intercession is
that no soul is
patched up. . .*

*"Men ought always to pray,
and not to faint."*
LUKE 18:1

The thing to watch in intercession is
that no soul is patched up;
a soul must get through into contact
with the life of God.

*"And He . . . wondered that
there was no intercessor."*
ISAIAH 59:16

Get into the real work of intercession,
and remember it is a work
that taxes every power;
but a work which has no snare.

Intimacy with Jesus

The one sign of discipleship is intimate connection with Him, a knowledge of Jesus Christ which nothing can shake.

"This kind can come forth by nothing, but by prayer and fasting."
MARK 9:29

We slander God by our very eagerness to work for Him without knowing Him.

"He calleth . . . by name." JOHN 10:3

The one sign of discipleship is intimate connection with Him, a knowledge of Jesus Christ which nothing can shake.

"When He had heard therefore that he was sick, He abode two days in the same place where he was."
JOHN 11:6

If Jesus Christ is bringing you into the understanding that prayer is for the glorifying of His Father, He will give you the first sign of His intimacy—silence.

Joy

*Joy means
the perfect
fulfillment
of that for
which I was
created and
regenerated. . .*

*". . .so that I might finish my course with joy,
and the ministry, which I have received
of the Lord Jesus."* ACTS 20:24

Joy means the perfect fulfillment of
that for which I was created and regenerated,
not the successful doing of a thing.

*"That My joy might remain in you, and that your
joy might be full."* JOHN 15:11

The joy of Jesus was the absolute self-surrender
and self-sacrifice of Himself to His Father,
the joy of doing that
which the Father sent Him to do.

"Take My yoke upon you, and learn of Me."
MATTHEW 11:29

The fact that the peace and the light
and the joy of God are there is proof
that the burden is there too.

71

Laziness

Take yourself by the scruff of the neck and shake off your incarnate laziness.

"While ye have light, believe in the light."
JOHN 12:36

If in a prayer meeting
God has shown you
something to do, don't say—
"I'll do it:" *do it!*
Take yourself by the scruff of the neck
and shake off your incarnate laziness.

"For all the promises of God in Him are yea, and in Him Amen."
2 CORINTHIANS 1:20

Lazy people always strike out
on an independent line.

Love

"I have called you friends."
JOHN 15:15

Love for God is not sentimental,
for the saint to love as God loves
is the most practical thing.

"Feed my sheep."
JOHN 21:17

And Jesus has some
extraordinarily funny sheep,
some bedraggled, dirty sheep,
some awkward, butting sheep,
some sheep that have gone astray!

"And to your brotherly kindness. . .charity."
2 PETER 1:7

God's love to me is inexhaustible,
and I must love others from the bedrock
of God's love to me.

God's love
to me is
inexhaustible,
and I must
love others
from the
bedrock of
God's love
to me.

Love

"Charity suffereth long, and is kind. . . ."
1 CORINTHIANS 13:4

Love is not premeditated, it is spontaneous, i.e.,
it bursts up in extraordinary ways.

*"Nay, in all these things we are more than
conquerors through Him that loved us."*
ROMANS 8:37

The bedrock of
our Christian faith is the unmerited,
fathomless marvel of the love
of God exhibited on the Cross of Calvary,
a love we never can and never shall merit.

*"That they may be one,
even as we are one."*
JOHN 17:22

Love is the outpouring of one personality
in fellowship with another personality.

Loyalty

Beware of anything that competes with loyalty to Jesus Christ.

" 'Let us go into Judea again.' His disciples say unto Him. . .'Goest thou thither again?' "
JOHN 11:7-8

Loyalty to Jesus means I have to step out where I do not see anything (cf. Matt. 14:29); loyalty to my notions means that I clear the ground first by my intelligence.

❧

"And we know that all things work together for good to them that love God."
ROMANS 8:28

To be faithful in every circumstance means that we have only one loyalty, and that is to our Lord.

❧

"Thomas answered and said unto Him, 'My Lord and my God.' "
JOHN 20:28

Beware of anything that competes with loyalty to Jesus Christ.

Loyalty

In a conflict of loyalty, obey Jesus Christ at all costs.

"Lord,
I will follow Thee
whithersoever Thou goest."
LUKE 9:57

In a conflict of loyalty,
obey Jesus Christ at all costs.

"None of us liveth to himself."
ROMANS 14:7

My life as a worker is the way I say "thank you"
to God for His unspeakable salvation.

New Birth

*When I am
born again,
the Spirit
of God. . .
identifies
me with
Jesus Christ.*

*"We have received. . .the spirit which is of God;
that we might know the things
that are freely given to us of God."*
1 CORINTHIANS 2:12

When I am born again,
the Spirit of God takes me right out of myself
and my experiences,
and identifies me with Jesus Christ.

❧

*"Behold, a virgin shall bring forth a son,
and they shall call His name Emmanuel,
which being interpreted is,
God with us."*
ISAIAH 7:14 (RV)

Just as Our Lord came into human history from
outside, so He must come into me from outside.
Have I allowed my personal human life to
become a "Bethlehem" for the Son of God?

❧

Now

Realize that the Lord is here now, and the emancipation is immediate.

"The God of Israel will be your rereward."
ISAIAH 52:12

Our present enjoyment of God's grace is
apt to be checked by the memory
of yesterday's sins and blunders. . . .
It is true that we have lost opportunities
which will never return,
but God can transform this destructive anxiety
into a constructive thoughtfulness. . .

*"Have I been so long time with you,
and yet hast thou not known Me, Philip?"*
JOHN 14:9

God never guides presently, but always now.
Realize that the Lord is here now,
and the emancipation is immediate.

"Be instant in season, out of season."
2 TIMOTHY 4:2

If we do only what we feel inclined to do,
some of us would do nothing forever and ever.

78

Now

The baptism of
the Holy Ghost
does not make
you think of
Time or
Eternity,
it is one
amazing
glorious
NOW.

*"We. . .beseech you also that ye receive
not the grace of God in vain."*
2 CORINTHIANS 6:1

Pray *now*; draw on the grace of God in the
moment of need. . . .Draw now, not presently.

*"Tarry ye in the city of Jerusalem,
until ye be endued with power from on high."*
LUKE 24:49

The baptism of the Holy Ghost does not
make you think of Time or Eternity,
it is one amazing glorious NOW.

*"Verily I say unto thee,
Thou shalt by no means come out thence,
till thou hast paid the uttermost farthing."*
MATTHEW 5:26

Do *now* what you will have to do some day.

Obedience

*Our Lord
never insists
upon
obedience;
He tells
us very
emphatically
what we ought
to do. . .*

*"If ye love Me,
ye will keep My commandments."*
JOHN 14:15 (RV)

Our Lord never insists upon obedience;
He tells us very emphatically what we ought to
do, but He never takes means to make us do it.

❦

"And he said, Who art Thou, Lord?"
ACTS 9:5

A man is a slave for obeying unless behind his
obedience there is a recognition of a holy God.

❦

*"By Myself have I sworn, saith the Lord,
for because thou hast done this thing . . .
that in blessing I will bless thee. . . ."*
GENESIS 22:16-17

There is no possibility of questioning when God
speaks if He speaks to His own nature in me;
prompt obedience is the only result.

Obedience

*Obey Him
with glad
reckless
joy.*

" 'Let us go into Judea again.'
His disciples say unto Him. . .
'Goest thou thither again?' "
JOHN 11:7-8

Obey Him with glad reckless joy.

⚥

"I thank Thee, O Father. . .
because Thou hast hid these things
from the wise and prudent,
and hast revealed them unto babes."
Matthew 11:25

The tiniest fragment of obedience,
and heaven opens and the profoundest
truths of God are yours straight away.

⚥

"Partakers of the divine nature."
2 PETER 1:4

. . .He will tax the last grain of sand and the
remotest star to bless us if we will obey Him.

Obedience

Any problem that comes between God and myself springs out of disobedience.

"Peace I leave with you,
My peace I give unto you: . . .
Let not your heart be troubled."
JOHN 14:27

Any problem that comes between
God and myself springs out of disobedience.

"If any man will do His will,
he shall know of the doctrine. . . ."
JOHN 7:17

At the risk of being fanatical
you must obey what God tells you.

"They laid hold upon one Simon. . .
and on him they laid the cross."
LUKE 23:26

If we obey God it is going to cost
other people more than it costs us,
and that is where the sting comes in.

"Who art Thou, Lord?"
ACTS 26:15

Have I been persecuting Jesus by a zealous
determination to serve Him in my own way?

*Obstinacy
and
self-will
will always
stab
Jesus Christ.*

❧

*"He charged them that they should
tell no man what things they had seen,
till the Son of man
were risen from the dead."*
MARK 9:9

An obstinate outlook will effectually
hinder God from revealing anything to us.

❧

"Saul, Saul, why persecutest thou Me?"
ACTS 26:14

Obstinacy and self-will
will always stab Jesus Christ.
It may hurt no one else, but it wounds His Spirit.

Oneness with God

Prayer is perfect and complete oneness with God.

"Saul, Saul, why persecutest thou Me?"
ACTS 26:14

All I do ought to be founded
on a perfect oneness with Him,
not on a self-willed determination to be godly.

"At that day ye shall ask in My name."
JOHN 16:26

The idea of prayer is not
in order to get answers from God;
prayer is perfect and complete oneness with God.

*"That they all may be one; as thou,
Father, art in me, and I in thee,
that they also may be one in us."*
JOHN 17:21

God will not leave us alone
until we are one with Him,
because Jesus has prayed that we may be.

Oneness with God

*"I do set my bow in the cloud,
and it shall be for a token of
a covenant between
Me and the earth."*
GENESIS 9:13

All the great blessings of God
are finished and complete,
but they are not mine until
I enter into relationship with Him
on the basis of His covenant.

❧

*"But have renounced the hidden things
of dishonesty."*
2 CORINTHIANS 4:2

Many have gone back because
they are afraid of looking at things
from God's standpoint.

❧

*God will not
leave us alone
until we are
one with Him,
because Jesus
has prayed
that we
may be.*

Patience

. . .patience conveys the idea of an immensely strong rock withstanding all onslaughts.

". . .An horror of great darkness fell upon him."
GENESIS 15:12

Never try and help God fulfill His word.

"When Jesus had made an end of commanding his twelve disciples, he departed thence to teach and to preach in their cities." MATTHEW 11:1

To wait is not to sit with folded hands,
but to learn to do what we are told.

"Be still, and know that I am God." PSALM 46:10

One of the greatest strains in life
is the strain of waiting for God.

"Though it tarry, wait for it." HABAKKUK 2:3

Patience is not indifference;
patience conveys the idea of an immensely strong
rock withstanding all onslaughts.

Peace

"Peace I leave with you,
My peace I give unto you."
JOHN 14:27

Reflected peace is the proof that you are
right with God because you are at liberty
to turn your mind to Him.
If you are not right with God,
you can never turn your mind
anywhere but on yourself.

"I came not to send peace, but a sword."
MATTHEW 10:34

Jesus Christ came to send a sword
through every peace that is not based on
a personal relationship to Himself.

Reflected
peace is the
proof that you
are right with
God because
you are at
liberty to turn
your mind
to Him.

Pouring Out

If we believe in Jesus, it is not what we gain, but what He pours through us that counts.

> "And. . .he pitched his tent,
> having Bethel on the west, and Hai on the east:
> and there he builded an altar."
> GENESIS 12:8

God will never let you hold a spiritual thing for yourself, it has to be given back to Him that He may make it a blessing to others.

> "He that believeth on Me. . .
> out of his belly shall flow. . . ."
> JOHN 7:38

If we believe in Jesus, it is not what we gain, but what He pours through us that counts.

> "We. . .beseech you also that ye receive
> not the grace of God in vain."
> 2 CORINTHIANS 6:1

Pour out the best you have, and always be poor. Never be diplomatic and careful about the treasure God gives. This is poverty triumphant.

Pouring Out

*Am I
willing to be
broken bread
and poured-out
wine for Him?*

"None of us liveth to himself."
ROMANS 14:7

Am I willing to be
broken bread and poured-out wine for Him?

∽

*". . .Nevertheless he would not drink thereof,
but poured it out unto the Lord."*
2 SAMUEL 23:16

If you have become bitter and sour,
it is because when God gave you a blessing
you clutched it for yourself;
whereas if you had poured it out unto the Lord,
you would have been
the sweetest person out of heaven.

∽

Prayer

The meaning of prayer is that we get hold of God, not of the answer.

"But we trusted. . .and beside all this, to day is the third day. . . ."
LUKE 24:21

The meaning of prayer is that we get hold of God, not of the answer.

"Lord, that I may receive my sight."
LUKE 18:41

If it is an impossibility,
it is the thing we have to ask. . . .
God will do the absolutely impossible.

"Pray without ceasing."
1 THESSALONIANS 5:17

God answers prayer in the best way,
not sometimes, but every time,
although the immediate manifestation of the
answer in the domain in which we want it
may not always follow.

*"We. . .beseech you also that ye receive
not the grace of God in vain."*
2 CORINTHIANS 6:1

Prayer is the exercise of
drawing on the grace of God.

"Pray without ceasing."
1 THESSALONIANS 5:17

If we think of prayer as the breath in our lung
and the blood from our hearts, we think rightly.
The blood flows ceaselessly,
and breathing continues ceaselessly;
we are not conscious of it, but it is always going on.

"At that day ye shall ask in My name."
JOHN 16:26

When prayer seems to be unanswered, beware of
trying to fix the blame on someone else. . . .
You will find there is a reason which is a deep
instruction to you, not to anyone else.

Prayer

It is not so true that "prayer changes things" as that prayer changes me and I change things.

"Wherefore take unto you the whole armour of God. . .praying always. . . ."
EPHESIANS 6:13, 18

If you ask me to pray for you and I am not complete in Christ, I may pray but it avails nothing; but if I am complete in Christ my prayer prevails all the time. Prayer is only effective when there is completeness—"Wherefore take unto you the whole armour of God."

"Lord, teach us to pray."
LUKE 11:1

It is not so true that "prayer changes things" as that prayer changes *me* and I change things.

"Shall I hide from Abraham that thing which I do?"
GENESIS 18:17

Keep praying in order to get a perfect understanding of God Himself.

Prayer

"And greater works than these shall he do;
because I go unto My Father."
JOHN 14:12

We look upon prayer as
a means of getting things for ourselves;
the Bible idea of prayer is
that we may get to know God Himself.

❧

"Lift up your eyes on high,
and behold who
hath created these things."
ISAIAH 40:26

One of the reasons of stultification in prayer
is that there is no imagination,
no power of putting ourselves
deliberately before God.

❧

. . .the Bible
idea of
prayer is
that we
may get
to know
God Himself.

Preaching

Our calling is not primarily to be holy men and women, but to be proclaimers of the Gospel of God. . . .

"Preach the word." 2 TIMOTHY 4:2

Let God have perfect liberty when you speak. Before God's message can liberate other souls, the liberation must be real in you. Gather your material, and set it alight when you speak.

"If that I may apprehend that for which also I am apprehended." PHILIPPIANS 3:12

When it comes to the call to preach, there must be the agonizing grip of God's hand on you, your life is in the grip of God for that one thing.

"Separated unto the gospel." ROMANS 1:1

Our calling is not primarily to be holy men and women, but to be proclaimers of the Gospel of God. . . . As long as our eyes are upon our own personal whiteness we shall never get near the reality of Redemption. . . . God cannot deliver me while my interest is merely in my own character.

Preaching

"For though I preach the gospel,
I have nothing to glory of:
for necessity is laid upon me;
yea, woe is unto me,
if I preach not the gospel!"
1 CORINTHIANS 9:16

Never water down the word of God,
preach it in its undiluted sternness. . .
But when you come to personal dealing
with your fellow men, remember who you are—
not a special being made up in heaven,
but a sinner saved by grace.

Remember
who you are——
not a
special being
made up in
heaven,
but a
sinner saved
by grace.

Pride

*Pride
is the
deification
of self. . .*

*"When they were alone,
He expounded all things to His disciples."*
MARK 4:34

The only way we can be of use to God
is to let Him take us through
the crooks and crannies of our own characters.

*"Master, where dwellest Thou? . . .
Come and see. . . . Follow Me."*
JOHN 1:38-39, 43

The disciple is one who
has the new name written all over him;
self-interest and pride and self-sufficiency
have been completely erased.

*"Master, where dwellest Thou? . . .
Come and see. . . . Follow Me."*
JOHN 1:38-39, 43

Pride is the deification of self. . .

Purity

*"We know not what
we should pray for as we ought:
but the Spirit itself
maketh intercession for us
with groanings
which cannot be uttered."*
ROMANS 8:26

Have we recognized that our body
is the temple of the Holy Ghost? If so,
we must be careful to keep it undefiled for Him.

*"Except your righteousness shall exceed
the righteousness of
the scribes and Pharisees,
ye shall in no case
enter into the kingdom of heaven."*
MATTHEW 5:20

The purity which God demands is impossible
unless I can be remade within,
and that is what Jesus has undertaken to do
by His Redemption.

*The purity
which God
demands is
impossible
unless
I can be
remade
within. . .*

Purity

*Purity is
the outcome of
sustained
spiritual
sympathy
with God.*

*"Follow righteousness, faith,
charity, peace,
with them that call
on the Lord out of a pure heart."*
2 TIMOTHY 2:22

Purity is not innocence, it is much more.
Purity is the outcome of
sustained spiritual sympathy with God.
We have to grow in purity.

*"Blessed are the pure in heart:
for they shall see God."*
MATTHEW 5:8

If we are going to retain personal contact with the
Lord Jesus Christ, it will mean there are some
things we must scorn to do or to think, some
legitimate things we must scorn to touch.

Purpose of God

"Ye shall be holy; for I am holy."
1 PETER 1:16 (RV)

God has one destined end for mankind,
viz., holiness.
His one aim is the production of saints.

"I, if I be lifted up from the earth,
will draw all men unto Me."
JOHN 12:32

We are sent by God to lift up Jesus Christ,
not to give wonderfully beautiful discourses.

"And greater works than these shall he do;
because I go unto My Father."
JOHN 14:12

Never allow the thought—
"I am of no use where I am";
because you certainly
can be of no use where you are not.

Purpose of God

God's ultimate purpose is that His Son might be manifested in my mortal flesh.

*"Jesus did not commit Himself unto them. . .
for He knew what was in men."*
JOHN 2:24-25

God's ultimate purpose is that
His Son might be manifested in my mortal flesh.

*"And straightway He constrained
His disciples to get into the ship,
and to go to the other side. . ."*
MARK 6:45

We must never put our dreams of success
as God's purpose for us;
His purpose may be exactly the opposite.

"My kingdom is not of this world."
JOHN 18:36

The central thing about the kingdom of Jesus
Christ is a personal relationship to Himself,
not public usefulness to men.

Putting God First

"For which of you,
intending to build a tower,
sitteth not down first, and counteth the cost,
whether he have sufficient to finish it?"
LUKE 14:28

Is God going to detect in His searching fire that
we have built on the foundation of Jesus
some enterprise of our own?

❧

"If God so clothe the grass of the field. . .
shall He not much more clothe you?"
MATTHEW 6:30

Am I continually separating myself to consider
God every day of my life?

❧

"Called to be saints."
1 CORINTHIANS 1:2

He must dominate.

Am I
continually
separating
myself to
consider God
every day of
my life?

Putting God First

Whenever we put other things first, there is confusion.

"Blessed are the poor in spirit."
MATTHEW 5:3

The phrase we hear so often,
Decide for Christ, is an emphasis
on something our Lord never trusted.
He never asks us to decide for Him,
but to yield to Him—a very different thing.

*"Take no thought for your life,
what ye shall eat, or what ye shall drink;
nor yet for your body ,what ye shall put on."*
MATTHEW 6:25

Whenever we put other things first,
there is confusion.

Redemption

"When it pleased God. . .to reveal His Son in me."
GALATIANS 1:15-16

The moral miracle of Redemption is
that God can put into me a new disposition
whereby I can live a totally new life.

"But ye are. . .a royal priesthood." *1 PETER 2:9*

Launch out in reckless belief that the Redemption
is complete, and then bother no more about
yourself, but begin to do as Jesus Christ said—
pray for the friend who comes to you at midnight,
pray for the saints, pray for all men.

*"Wherefore, as by one man
sin entered into the world, and death by sin;
and so death passed upon all men,
for that all have sinned."*
ROMANS 5:12

Sin is a thing I am born with and I cannot touch
it; God touches sin in Redemption.

Sin is a thing I am born with and I cannot touch it; God touches sin in Redemption.

Redemption

The only thing that safeguards is the Redemption of Jesus Christ.

"I am debtor both to the Greeks, and to the Barbarians." ROMANS 1:14

Every bit of my life that is of value I owe to the Redemption of Jesus Christ; am I doing anything to enable Him to bring His Redemption into actual manifestation in other lives?

"But the natural man receiveth not the things of the Spirit of God: for they are foolishness unto him." 1 CORINTHIANS 2:14

Nothing can satisfy the need but that which created the need. This is the meaning of Redemption— it creates and it satisfies.

"Out of the heart proceed. . ." MATTHEW 15:19

The only thing that safeguards is the Redemption of Jesus Christ.

Regeneration

*I am a
child of
God only by
regeneration. . .*

*"And if thy right hand offend thee,
cut it off, and cast it from thee:
for it is profitable for thee that one
of thy members should perish, and not that
thy whole body should be cast into hell."*
MATTHEW 5:30

When God alters a man by regeneration,
the characteristic of the life to begin with is
that it is maimed.

"Lord, that I may receive my sight." LUKE 18:41

The most impossible thing to you is that
you should be so identified with the Lord
that there is nothing of the old life left.
He will do it if you ask Him.

*"Or what man is there of you, whom if his son
ask bread, will he give him a stone?"*
MATTHEW 7:9

I am a child of God only by regeneration. . .

Reliance

*The attitude
must be one
of complete
reliance
on God.*

*"For the time is come
that judgment must begin
at the house of God."*
1 PETER 4:17

Every element of self-reliance must be slain
by the power of God.

*"Peace I leave with you,
My peace I give unto you: . . .
Let not your heart be troubled."*
JOHN 14:27

The attitude must be
one of complete reliance on God.

"Sir, Thou hast nothing to draw with."
JOHN 4:11

We are rather hurt at the idea that
He can do what we cannot.

Reliance

Have you the slightest reliance on anything other than God?

"Ye cannot serve the Lord."
JOSHUA 24:19

Have you the slightest reliance
on anything other than God?

&

*"And Peter. . .walked on the water to go
to Jesus. But when he saw the
wind boisterous, he was afraid."*
MATTHEW 14:29-30

Let actual circumstances be what they may,
keep recognizing Jesus, maintain
complete reliance on Him.

&

*"Peace I leave with you, My peace I give unto
you: . . .Let not your heart be troubled."*
JOHN 14:27

As long as we try to serve two ends, ourselves
and God, there is perplexity. The attitude must
be one of complete reliance on God.

Repentance

Repentance does not bring a sense of sin, but a sense of unutterable unworthiness.

"For godly sorrow worketh repentance to salvation."
2 CORINTHIANS 7:10

The bedrock of Christianity is repentance.

"I indeed baptize you with water. . . but He. . .shall baptize you with the Holy Ghost, and with fire."
MATTHEW 3:11

Repentance does not bring a sense of sin, but a sense of unutterable unworthiness.

"For by one offering he hath perfected for ever them that are sanctified."
HEBREWS 10:14

Our repentance is merely the outcome of our personal realization of the Atonement which He has worked out for us.

Resurrection Life

"Ye must be born again."
JOHN 3:7

To be born of God means that I have
the supernatural power of God to stop sinning.

❧

"And Abraham built an altar. . .
and bound Isaac his son."
GENESIS 22:9

God nowhere tells us to
give up things for the sake of giving them up.
He tells us to give them up for the sake of the
only thing worth having—viz., life with Himself.

❧

"Only in the throne will I be greater than thou."
GENESIS 41:40

I have to account to God for the way in which
I rule my body under His domination. . . .
Every saint can have his body
under absolute control for God.

Resurrection Life

*Many a
Christian
worker has left
Jesus Christ. . .
The reason
for this is the
absence of the
resurrection
life of Jesus.*

*" 'By this we believe'. . . .Jesus answered,
'Do ye now believe?' "*
JOHN 16:30-31

Many a Christian worker has left Jesus Christ
alone and gone into work from a sense of duty,
or from a sense of need arising out
of his own particular discernment.
The reason for this is the absence of
the resurrection life of Jesus.

"All my fresh springs shall be in Thee."
PSALM 87:7 (PBV)

But as we bring every bit of our bodily life
into harmony with the new life which God
has put in us, He will exhibit in us the virtues
that were characteristic of the Lord Jesus.

110

Right Relationship

*"Shall I hide from
Abraham that thing which I do?"*
GENESIS 18:17

When you are rightly related to God, it is a life of
freedom and liberty and delight, you are God's
will, and all your common-sense decisions are
His will for you unless He checks.

"Being justified freely by His grace. . ."
ROMANS 3:24

We have to realize that we cannot
earn or win anything from God;
we must either receive it as a gift or do without it.

*"The water that I shall give him
shall be in him a well of water."*
JOHN 4:14

Some of us are like the Dead Sea,
always taking in but never giving out,
because we are not rightly related to the Lord Jesus.

Sacrifice

The only way in which we can offer a spiritual sacrifice to God is by presenting our bodies a living sacrifice.

*"Abraham had two sons,
the one by a bondmaid,
the other by a freewoman."*
GALATIANS 4:22

The only way in which we can offer a spiritual sacrifice to God is by presenting our bodies a living sacrifice.

*"And they that are Christ's
have crucified the flesh with
the affections and lusts."*
GALATIANS 5:24

The natural life is not spiritual,
and it can only be made spiritual by sacrifice.
If we do not resolutely sacrifice the natural,
the supernatural can never become natural in us.

Sainthood

"To him that overcometh. . ."
REVELATION 2:7

No man is virtuous because he cannot help it;
virtue is acquired.

∽

*"Yea, and if I be offered upon
the sacrifice and service of your faith,
I joy, and rejoice with you all."*
PHILIPPIANS 2:17

Some saints cannot do menial work and remain
saints because it is beneath their dignity.

∽

"I was not disobedient unto the heavenly vision."
ACTS 26:19

Watch God's cyclones.
The only way God sows His saints
is by His whirlwind. . . . Let God fling you out,
and do not go until He does. . . .
If God sows you, you will bring forth fruit.

*The only way
God sows
His saints
is by His
whirlwind. . . .*

Sainthood

A saint's life is in the hands of God.

> *"Master,*
> *where dwellest Thou?. . .*
> *Come and see. . . .*
> *Follow Me."*
> JOHN 1:38-39, 43

Why are you not a saint?
It is either that you do not want to be a saint,
or that you do not believe God can make you one.

> *"Because thou hast kept*
> *the word of My patience."*
> REVELATION 3:10

A saint's life is in the hands of God
like a bow and arrow in the hands of an archer.
God is aiming at something the saint cannot see,
and He stretches and strains,
and every now and again the saint says—
"I cannot stand any more." God does not heed,
He goes on stretching till His purpose is in sight,
then He lets fly.

Sainthood

"Let them that suffer
according to the will of God
commit the keeping of their souls
to Him in well doing."
1 PETER 4:19

God places
His saints
in the most
useless
places.

God places His saints in the most useless places.

❧

"Whatsoever ye do, do all to the glory of God."
1 CORINTHIANS 10:31

The test of the life of a saint is not success,
but faithfulness in human life
as it actually is.

❧

Sanctification

Am I willing to let Jesus be made sanctification to me, . . .

"Walk while ye have the light, lest darkness come upon you."
JOHN 12:35

If you *say* you are sanctified, *show* it.
The experience must be so genuine that it is shown in the life.

"This is the will of God, even your sanctification."
1 THESSALONIANS 4:3

Am I willing to let Jesus
be made sanctification to me,
and to let the life of Jesus
be manifested in my mortal flesh?

"And the very God of peace sanctify you wholly."
1 THESSALONIANS 5:23-24

Sanctification means being made one with Jesus
so that the disposition that ruled Him will rule us
. . . .It will cost everything that is not of God in us.

Sanctification

"Abraham had two sons,
the one by a bondmaid,
the other by a freewoman."
GALATIANS 4:22

Sanctification means
more than deliverance from sin,
it means the deliberate commitment of myself
whom God has saved to God,
and that I do not care what it costs.

"And my speech and my preaching
was not with enticing words
of man's wisdom,
but in demonstration of the
Spirit and of power."
1 Corinthians 2:4

I have deliberately to give
my sanctified life to God for His service,
so that He can use me
as His hands and feet.

Sanctification
means . . . the
deliberate
commitment of
myself whom
God has saved
to God and that
I do not care
what it costs.

Sanctification

Sanctification
is "Christ
in you". . .

*"Of Him are ye in Christ Jesus,
who of God is made unto us. . .
sanctification."*
1 CORINTHIANS 1:30

Sanctification is "Christ in you". . .
Sanctification means
the impartation of the qualities
of Jesus Christ.

"All my fresh springs shall be in Thee."
PSALM 87:7 (PBV)

Watch how God will wither up your confidence in
natural virtues after sanctification,
and in any power you have,
until you learn to draw your life from the
reservoir of the resurrection life of Jesus.

Self-Pity

*If we look
for justice,
we will begin
to grouse and
to indulge in
the discontent
of self-pity.*

*"For Christ sent me not to baptize,
but to preach the gospel."*
1 CORINTHIANS 1:17

When we touch the bedrock of the reality of the
Gospel of God, we shall never bother God any
further with little personal plaints.

∝

"And I will give you rest."
MATTHEW 11:28

Beware of allowing self-consciousness
to continue because by slow degrees it will
awaken self-pity, and self-pity is Satanic.

∝

*"I am with thee to deliver thee,
saith the Lord."*
JEREMIAH 1:8

If we look for justice, we will begin to grouse
and to indulge in the discontent of self-pity—
Why should I be treated like this?

Self-Pity

No sin is worse than the sin of self-pity.

"Partakers of the divine nature."
2 PETER 1:4

What does it matter
if external circumstances are hard?
Why should they not be!
If we give way to self-pity
and indulge in the luxury of misery,
we banish God's riches from our own lives and
hinder others from entering into His provision.
No sin is worse than the sin of self-pity,
because it obliterates God and
puts self-interest upon the throne.

"Fellow labourer in the gospel of Christ."
1 THESSALONIANS 3:2

Self-pity is of the devil;
if I go off on that line I cannot be used
by God for His purpose in the world.

Self-Realization

"Therefore if thou bring thy gift to the altar,
and there rememberest that thy brother hath
ought against thee; leave there thy gift before the
altar, and go thy way; first be reconciled to thy
brother, and then come and offer thy gift."
MATTHEW 5:23-24

. . .My right to myself—
the thing God intends you to give up if ever you
are going to be a disciple of Jesus Christ.

"Seek, and ye shall find." LUKE 11:9

If you ask for things from life instead of from God,
you ask amiss, i.e.,
you ask from a desire for self-realization.
The more you realize yourself
the less will you seek God.

"That I may know Him." PHILIPPIANS 3:10

Self-realization leads to
the enthronement of work.

*Self-
realization
leads to the
enthronement
of work.*

121

Self-Realization

Thoughts about myself hinder my usefulness to God.

"I remember. . .the kindness of thy youth."
JEREMIAH 2:2

Am I so in love with Him
that I take no account of where I go?
or am I watching for the respect due to me;
weighing how much service I ought to give?

*"If God so clothe the grass of the field. . .
shall He not much more clothe you?"*
MATTHEW 6:30

"Consider the lilies of the field"—
they grow where they are put.
Many of us refuse to grow where we are put,
consequently we take root nowhere.

*"Not as though I had already attained,
either were already perfect. . ."*
PHILIPPIANS 3:12

Thoughts about myself
hinder my usefulness to God.

"Building up yourselves on your most holy faith."
JUDE 20

It is inbred in us that we have to do exceptional
things for God; but we have not. We have to be
exceptional in the ordinary things. . . .

*"Who now rejoice in my sufferings for you,
and fill up that which is behind of the afflictions
of Christ in my flesh for His body's sake."*
COLOSSIANS 1:24

We must never choose
the scene of our own martyrdom.

*"Though the more abundantly I love you,
the less I be loved."*
2 CORINTHIANS 12:15

His idea is that we serve Him
by being the servants of other men.
Jesus Christ out-socialists the socialists.

*We must
never choose
the scene
of our own
martyrdom.*

Service

*Suppose
God wants to
teach you to
say, "I know
how to be
abased"?*

*"Yea, and if I be offered upon the sacrifice
and service of your faith,
I joy, and rejoice with you all."*
PHILIPPIANS 2:17

Suppose God wants to teach you to say,
"I know how to be abased"?
—are you ready to be offered up like that?
Are you ready to be
not so much as a drop in a bucket. . . ?

*"If I then, your Lord and Master,
have washed your feet,
ye also ought to wash one another's feet."*
JOHN 13:14

The things that Jesus did were of the most
menial and commonplace order,
and this is an indication that it takes
all God's power in me to do the most
commonplace things in His way.

Simplicity

Simplicity is the secret of seeing things clearly.

*"Have I been so long time with you,
and yet hast thou not known Me, Philip?"*
JOHN 14:9

It is opinions of our own which make us stupid;
when we are simple we are never stupid,
we discern all the time.

"The simplicity that is in Christ."
2 CORINTHIANS 11:3

Simplicity is the secret of seeing things clearly.

*"And all things that are written by
the prophets concerning the Son of Man
shall be accomplished. . . . And they
understood none of these things."*
LUKE 18:31, 34

If we have a purpose of our own,
it destroys the simplicity and the leisureliness
which ought to characterize the children of God.

Sin

No man knows what sin is until he is born again.

"A man of sorrows, and acquainted with grief."
ISAIAH 53:3

Either God or sin must die in my life.

*"If we walk in the light, as He is in the light. . .
the blood of Jesus Christ His Son
cleanseth us from all sin."*
1 JOHN 1:7

No man knows what sin is until he is born again.
Sin is what Jesus Christ faced on Calvary.

*"Casting down imaginations, and
every high thing that exalteth itself against
the knowledge of God."*
2 CORINTHIANS 10:5

The warfare is not against sin; we can never fight
against sin: Jesus Christ deals with sin in
Redemption. The conflict is along the line of
turning our natural life into a spiritual life.

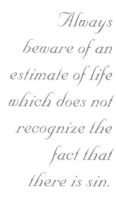

Sin

Always beware of an estimate of life which does not recognize the fact that there is sin.

"Ye must be born again."
JOHN 3:7

First John 3:9 does not mean that we cannot sin; it means that if we obey the life of God in us, we need not sin.

"This is your hour, and the power of darkness."
LUKE 22:53

Always beware of an estimate of life which does not recognize the fact that there is sin.

"For we must all appear before the judgment seat of Christ."
2 CORINTHIANS 5:10

No struggling nor praying will enable you to stop doing some things, and the penalty of sin is that gradually you get used to it and do not know that it is sin.

Spiritual Poverty

The knowledge of our own poverty brings us to the moral frontier where Jesus Christ works.

"But we trusted. . .and beside all this, to day is the third day. . ."
LUKE 24:21

Anything that savours of dejection spiritually is always wrong. If depression and oppression visit me, I am to blame; God is not, nor is anyone else.

"Being justified freely by His grace. . ."
ROMANS 3:24

The greatest blessing spiritually is the knowledge that we are destitute; until we get there Our Lord is powerless. . . . It is only when we get hungry spiritually that we receive the Holy Spirit.

"Blessed are the poor in spirit."
MATTHEW 5:3

The knowledge of our own poverty brings us to the moral frontier where Jesus Christ works.

Spiritual Stagnation

"All my fresh springs shall be in Thee."
PSALM 87:7 (PBV)

*. . . .Learn to
draw your life
from the
reservoir of the
resurrection
life of Jesus.*

. . . .Learn to draw your life from the reservoir of the resurrection life of Jesus. Thank God if you are going through a drying-up experience!

❧

*"Lord, and what shall this man do?. . .
What is that to thee? Follow thou Me."*
JOHN 21:21-22

If there is stagnation spiritually, never allow it to go on, but get into God's presence and find out the reason for it.

❧

*"Let us consider one another to provoke
unto love and to good works;
not forsaking the assembling
of ourselves together."*
HEBREWS 10:24-25

We want to use prayer and Bible reading for the purpose of retirement.

Suffering

"If Thou canst do any thing, have compassion on us, and help us."
MARK 9:22

It is in the valley that we have to live for the glory of God.

"Let them that suffer according to the will of God, commit the keeping of their souls to Him in well doing."
1 PETER 4:19

To choose to suffer means that there is something wrong; to choose God's will even if it means suffering is a very different thing. No healthy saint ever chooses suffering; he chooses God's will, as Jesus did. . .

Suffering

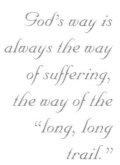

God's way is always the way of suffering, the way of the "long, long trail."

"What shall I say? Father, save me from this hour? But for this cause came I unto this hour. Father, glorify Thy name."
JOHN 12:27-28 (RV)

Sin and sorrow and suffering *are,*
and it is not for us to say that God has made a mistake in allowing them.

"In the world ye shall have tribulation: but be of good cheer; I have overcome the world."
JOHN 16:33

If there is no strain, there is no strength.

"Rejoice, inasmuch as ye are partakers of Christ's sufferings."
1 PETER 4:13

God's way is always the way of suffering, the way of the "long, long trail."

Temptation

The temptation fits the nature of the one tempted, and reveals the possibilities of the nature.

"Ye are they which have continued with Me in My temptations."
LUKE 22:28

The temptations of Jesus continued throughout His earthly life, and they will continue throughout the life of the Son of God in us.

"There hath no temptation taken you but such as is common to man."
1 CORINTHIANS 10:13

A man's disposition on the inside, i.e., what he possesses in his personality, determines what he is tempted by on the outside. The temptation fits the nature of the one tempted, and reveals the possibilities of the nature.

Tribulation

*"And as they followed,
they were afraid."*
MARK 10:32

When the darkness of dismay comes,
endure until it is over,
because out of it will come
that following of Jesus
which is an unspeakable joy.

❦

"Arise and eat."
1 KINGS 19:5

If we were never depressed
we should not be alive;
it is the nature of a crystal
never to be depressed.
A human being is capable of depression,
otherwise there would be
no capacity for exaltation.

❦

Tribulation

Let tribulation be what it may. . .it is not able to separate us from the love of God.

*"Nay, in all these things
we are more than conquerors
through Him that loved us."*
ROMANS 8:37

The surf that distresses the ordinary swimmer
produces in the surf-rider the super-joy
of going clean through it.
Apply that to our own circumstances,
these very things—tribulation,
distress, persecution, produce in us the
super-joy; they are not things to fight.

*"Who shall separate us
from the love of Christ?"*
ROMANS 8:35

Let tribulation be what it may—
exhausting, galling, it is not able to separate us
from the love of God.

Trust

Never trust anything but the grace of God in yourself or in anyone else.

"Jesus did not commit Himself unto them. . . for He knew what was in men."
JOHN 2:24-25

Never trust anything but the grace of God in yourself or in anyone else.

"Be still, and know that I am God."
PSALM 46:10

The greatest fear a man has is not that he will be damned, but that Jesus Christ will be worsted, that the things He stood for— love and justice and forgiveness and kindness among men—will not win out in the end. . . . God is not going to be worsted.

"Jesus did not commit Himself unto them. . . for He knew what was in man."
JOHN 2:24-25

If our trust is placed in human beings, we shall end in despairing of everyone.

Trust

You cannot lay up for a rainy day if you are trusting Jesus Christ.

"If any man be in Christ, he is a new creature: old things are passed away."
2 CORINTHIANS 5:17

Have we come to the place where
God can withdraw His blessings and
it does not affect our trust in Him?

"Commit thy way unto the Lord;
trust also in Him;
and He shall bring it to pass."
PSALM 37:5

You cannot lay up for a rainy day if you
are trusting Jesus Christ.

Utmost

The only way to be obedient to the heavenly vision is to give our utmost for God's highest.

"Behold, as the eyes of servants look unto the hand of their masters. . . so our eyes wait upon the Lord our God."
PSALM 123:2

We have to realize that no effort can be too high.

"While ye have light, believe in the light."
JOHN 12:36

We must bring our commonplace life up to the standard revealed in the high hour.

"I was not disobedient unto the heavenly vision."
ACTS 26:19

The only way to be obedient to the heavenly vision is to give our utmost for God's highest, and this can only be done by continually and resolutely recalling the vision.

137

Value to God

The comradeship of God is made up out of men who know their poverty.

"Then He took unto Him the twelve."
LUKE 18:31

The comradeship of God is made up
out of men who know their poverty.
He can do nothing with the man who thinks
that he is of use to God.

*"Behold the fowls of the air. . . .
Consider the lilies of the field."*
MATTHEW 6:26, 28

If you want to be of use to God,
get rightly related to Jesus Christ and He will
make you of use unconsciously every minute you
live.

"I remember. . .the kindness of thy youth."
JEREMIAH 2:2

It is a great thing to think that Jesus Christ has
need of me, "Give Me to drink."

Value to God

"And Abraham built an altar. . .
and bound Isaac his son."
GENESIS 22:9

It is of no value to God to give Him
your life for death. He wants you to be a *"living*
sacrifice," to let Him have all your powers that
have been saved and sanctified through Jesus.

"Wherefore we labour that. . .
we may be accepted of Him."
2 CORINTHIANS 5:9

My worth to God in public
is what I am in private.

"She hath wrought a good work on Me."
MARK 14:6

It is never a question of being of use,
but of being of value to God Himself.

It is never a
question of
being of use,
but of being of
value to God
Himself.

Vision

When God gives a vision, transact business on that line, no matter what it costs.

*"Have mercy upon us,
O Lord, have mercy upon us:
for we are exceedingly filled with contempt."*
PSALM 123:3

It is extraordinary what an enormous power
there is in simple things
to distract our attention from God.

"Did not our heart burn within us?"
LUKE 24:32

When God gives a vision, transact business on
that line, no matter what it costs.

*"Where there is no vision,
the people cast off restraint."*
PROVERBS 29:18 (RV)

. . . .Wherever there is vision,
there is also a life of rectitude because the vision
imparts moral incentive.

"I was not disobedient unto the heavenly vision."
ACTS 26:19

We cannot attain to a vision, we must live in the
inspiration of it until it accomplishes itself. We
get so practical that we forget the vision.

"And the parched ground shall become a pool."
ISAIAH 35:7

If you have ever had the vision of God, you may
try as you like to be satisfied on a lower level, but
God will never let you.

"Enoch walked with God."
GENESIS 5:24

God's Spirit alters the atmosphere of our way
of looking at things, and things begin
to be possible which never were possible before.

Worry

Have you ever noticed what Jesus said would choke the word He puts in?. . . It is the little worries always.

"Take no thought for your life, what ye shall eat, or what ye shall drink; nor yet for your body, what ye shall put on."
MATTHEW 6:25

Have you ever noticed what Jesus said would choke the word He puts in? The devil? No, the cares of this world. It is the little worries always.

"How much more shall your Father which is in heaven give good things to them that ask Him?"
MATTHEW 7:11

. . . .God is my Father, He loves me,
I shall never think of anything
He will forget, why should I worry?

"He went out, not knowing whither he went."
HEBREWS 11:8

Suppose God is the God you know Him to be
when you are nearest to Him—
what an impertinence worry is!